FLORA

Garden Journal

FLORA

Garden Journal

January

1

2

3

4

Above: Camellia jap-
onica *'Candy Apple'*
is a popular garden
shrub admired for
its lovely flowers.

Opposite page: Many
plants offer year-round
interest, with seasonal
displays of colorful foli-
age, flowers, and fruits.

5

6

7

8

9

10

11

Right: Adenophora polyantha *features pendent bell-shaped flowers in a rich shade of purple-blue.*

Opposite page: The pink and mauve blooms of Clematis *'Fireworks' are up to 8 in (20 cm) wide.*

12

13

14

15

16

17

18

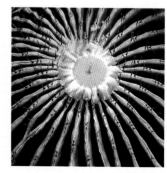

Right: Echinocactus platyacanthus *is a species from Mexico that bursts into bloom from spring to autumn.*

Opposite page: Primula auriculata *'Jeannie Telford'. Primulas are colorful, easy to grow, and widely available.*

January

19

20

21

22

23

24

25

26

27

28

29

30

31

Right: Dahlia *'Herald-ine' is a Semi-cactus dahlia with large pink flowerheads that are ideal for arrangements.*

February

1

2

3

4

*Above: From southern
Africa,* Moraea villosa
*has delicate pale purple
iris-like flowers with
bold blue centers.*

Opposite page: Iris
*'Purple Rain', like all
iris cultivars, needs a
sunny position with
protection from wind.*

February

5

6

7

8

9

10

11

12

13

14

15

16

17

18

Right: Meconopsis grandis, *also known as the Himalayan blue poppy, bears rich blue flowers in summer.*

19

20

21

22

23

24

25

Right: The mountain ash from Australia (Eucalyptus regnans) is the tallest hardwood tree in the world.

Opposite page: Tagetes patula *'Jolly Jester' is aptly named, due to its brightly colored red and yellow flowers.*

26

27

28

29

Right: Papaver nudi-
caule *'Meadhome's
Strain' has yellow and
orange flowers that
appear in spring.*

Opposite page: Chrys-
anthemum *'Yellow
Biarritz' is a Spoon-
shaped chrysanthemum
perfect for exhibition.*

March

1

2

3

4

*Above: 'James Galway'
is a Modern Shrub rose
named for the talented
musician. It has soft
pink flowers.*

Opposite page: Rhodo-
dendron *'Christine'*
*has magenta flowers
complemented by rich
dark green leaves.*

5

6

7

8

9

10

11

Right: Epacris longi-flora *is an adaptable Australian shrub with white-tipped, pinkish red, tubular flowers.*

Opposite page: The Mandevilla sanderi *bears gorgeous, yellow-throated, scarlet-pink blooms.*

March

12

13

14

15

16

17

18

Previous page: Camellia reticulata; 'Dali Cha'

19

20

21

22

23

24

25

Right: Rhododendron *'Shin Utena'. The plants in this genus are loved for their masses of colorful flowers.*

26

27

28

29

30

31

Right: Zinnia elegans
is a native of Mexico.
It has produced a large
number of cultivars in
a wide range of colors.

Opposite page: Rosa,
Modern, Cluster-
flowered (Floribunda),
'Woburn Abbey' is a
good repeat flowerer.

April

1

2

3

4

Above: Nelumbo
'Carolina Queen' is a
hardy lotus producing
single pink blossoms
with a yellow center.

Opposite page: There
are thousands of shrubs
available, which can
contribute color and
interest to a garden.

5

6

7

8

9

10

11

Right: Native to central eastern Australia, macadamia plants are cultivated for their hard-shelled nuts.

Opposite page: Tulips are especially delightful when planted in a massed bed of a single type or color.

12

13

14

15

16

17

18

Right: Primula sieboldii *produces white, pink, or purple flowers from spring to early summer.*

Opposite page: 'Copthorne' is a Unique/ Scented-leafed Pelargonium *with striking bicolored flowers.*

May

❧

1
_____

2
_____

3
_____

Above: Tigridia
pavonia *is a flam-*
boyant Mexican native
with triangular flowers
and iris-like foliage.

4
_____

Opposite page: The
crinkly flowers of
Papaver rupifragum
are orange to scarlet,
and bloom in summer.

Previous page: Asler novae-angliaea

May

5

6

7

8

9

10

11

12

13

14

15

16

17

18

Right: Lilium 'Salmon Queen' has pale orange bowl-shaped flowers that add charm to a summer garden.

19

20

21

22

23

24

25

Right: Nigella damas-
cena *is also called "love
in a mist" or "devil in
a bush," and bears
lilac-blue flowers.*

*Opposite page: Com-
monly known as "hen
and chicks,"* Echeveria
elegans *is a moderately
frost-hardy succulent.*

26

27

28

29

30

31

Right: Dracaena reflexa *'Song of India' is a variegated form with broad creamy white leaf margins.*

Opposite page: 'Yellow Heaven' is one of the many Paeonia suffruticosa *cultivars that are available.*

June

1

2

3

4

Above: The pure white flowers of Scabiosa caucasica *'Alba' have a dense pincushion-like center.*

Opposite page: Rhododendron *'Sunburst' is valued for its vibrant crimson flowers and rich green foliage.*

5

6

7

8

9

10

11

Right: Echinops bannaticus *'Taplow Blue' has bright blue-purple flowers and woolly gray stems.*

Opposite page: As the name indicates, Iris douglasiana *'Oregonensis' comes from the Pacific Northwest.*

June

12

13

14

15

16

17

18

19

20

21

22

23

24

25

*Right: 'Penny Blue'
and 'Penny Orange'
are just two of the
delightful cultivars
of* Viola cornuta.

26

27

28

29

30

Right: Along North Carolina's Blue Ridge Parkway you'll see a brilliant display of autumn color.

Opposite page: The waratah (Telopea speciosissima) *is one of the most popular Australian wildflowers.*

July

1

2

3

4

Above: 'Blue Nile' is an exquisite Large-flowered (Hybrid Tea) rose with delicate lavender-blue flowers.

Opposite page: The daisy-like Erigeron peregrinus *grows wild in San Juan National Forest, Colorado, USA.*

5

6

7

8

9

10

11

Right: Several pink and apricot forms of Grevillea banksii *are available, such as the attractive 'Misty Pink'.*

Opposite page: 'Antilope' is a Rhododendron, Deciduous Azalea *hybrid with fragrant pink flowers.*

12

13

14

15

16

17

18

Right: Gazania *'Black-berry Ripple' is the perfect plant to add color and interest to a seaside garden.*

Opposite page: 'Yellow Dawn', a tulip from the Greigii Group, has golden yellow flowers with a deep red base.

August

1

2

3

4

Above: Cultivars of
Camellia japonica,
such as the tricolored
'Anita', are favored in
ornamental gardens.

Opposite page: Exten-
sive violet veining
marks the lighter color
petals of the award
winning Iris ensata.

August

5

6

7

8

9

10

11

12

13

14

15

16

17

18

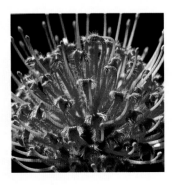

Right: Leucospermum tottum *'Scarlet Rib-bon' is a compact rounded shrub that flowers in late spring.*

19

20

21

22

23

24

25

Right: 'White Gish' is a Rhododendron, Rutherford Indica *Azalea valued for its pristine white flowers.*

Opposite page: Pelargonium *'Pacevka'. Dried pelargonium leaves are often added to potpourri.*

26

27

28

29

30

31

Right: Cultivars of
Primula auriculata
come in some unusual
color combinations, as
seen in 'Hawkwood'.

Opposite page: The
scent of Rosa, Modern,
Modern Shrub, 'Anna
Zinkeisen' *is similar to*
that of new-mown hay.

September

1

2

3

4

*Above: 'White Swan',
a cultivar of* Echinacea
purpurea, *has fragrant
daisy-like flowers ideal
for a meadow garden.*

*Opposite page: There
are many cultivars of*
Schizanthus × wise-
tonensis, *all having
speckled yellow throats.*

September

5

6

7

8

9

10

11

Right: Known as the Greek maple, Acer heldreichii *has winged fruits that are 1–2 in (2.5–5 cm) long.*

Opposite page: 'Coral Beauty' is one of the many Zinnia *cultivars that will add brilliance to a summer garden.*

September

26

27

28

29

30

Right: The needle-like blue-green leaves of the Bhutan pine, Pinus wallichiana, *are up to 8 in (20 cm) long.*

Opposite page: Pelargonium *'Brunswick' is grown for its fragrant leaves as well as for the attractive flowers.*

October

1

2

3

4

Above: 'Coronation
Gold' is a Cluster-
flowered (Floribunda)
rose that blooms in
summer and autumn.

Opposite page: Lilium,
Oriental Hybrid,
'Royal Sunset' adds
color and fragrance to
the garden in summer.

5

6

7

8

9

10

11

Right: The Chinese plumbago, Cerato-stigma willmottianum, *is a deciduous shrub with lilac-blue flowers.*

*Opposite page: The waratah (*Telopea speciosissima*) is a well known Australian spring wildflower.*

12

13

14

15

16

17

18

Right: Rhododendron
'George Bugden' is a
good cultivar if you
want to bring bright-
ness to the garden.

Opposite page: Known
as the Ohio buckeye,
Aesculus glabra *has*
prickly seed capsules
and rough bark.

November

1

2

3

4

Above: Rosa, Modern, Cluster-flowered (Flori-bunda), 'Rustica' produces lightly scented peach-yellow flowers.

Opposite page: The flowers of Nymphaea cacrulea *'Colorata' open in the day and close at night.*

19

20

21

22

23

24

25

Right: Lonicera ×
purpusii *is a semi-
deciduous shrub that
produces fragrant
creamy white flowers.*

*Opposite page: In a
meadow garden, there
is plenty of scope to
combine a variety of
colors and textures.*

26

27

28

29

30

Right: The unopened buds of the Capparis spinosa *flower are pickled in brine and eaten as capers.*

Opposite page: Magnolia 'Heaven Scent' *produces soft pink flowers that indeed have a glorious scent.*

December

1

2

3

Above: Camellia *'Night Rider' bears small semi-double blooms in a dramatic shade of black-red.*

Opposite page: The orange cultivar 'David Howard' is a member of the Decorative dahlia group.

4

5

6

7

8

9

10

11

Right: Pelargonium
'Ardwick Cinnamon'
*has soft pink flowers
with deep maroon-red
markings.*

*Opposite page: 'Cap-
tain Starlight', like
all the Angel pelar-
goniums, has masses
of single flowers.*

December

26

27

28

29

30

31

Right: Eucalyptus
pachyphylla *is often
found in the red sands
of Australia and suits
hot dry climates.*

Opposite page: Rosa,
*Modern, Cluster-
flowered (Floribunda),
'Cathedral' is a hardy
disease-resistant rose.*

Planting Record

....

....

....

....

....

....

....

....

....

....

....

....

....

....

Planting Record

Planting Record

....

....

....

....

....

....

....

....

....

....

....

....

....

....

....

Planting Record

....

....

....

....

....

....

....

....

....

....

....

....

....

....

....

....

Garden Plans

Garden Plans

Garden Plans

Garden Plans

Rainfall Record

Rainfall Record

Notes

Notes

Addresses

Name . . . . Telephone . . . .
Address. . . . . Mobile . . . .
. . . . Email . . . .
. . . . Pager . . . .
. . . . Fax . . . .

Name . . . . Telephone . . . .
Address. . . . . Mobile . . . .
. . . . Email . . . .
. . . . Pager . . . .
. . . . Fax . . . .

Name . . . . Telephone . . . .
Address. . . . . Mobile . . . .
. . . . Email . . . .
. . . . Pager . . . .
. . . . Fax . . . .

Name . . . . Telephone . . . .
Address. . . . . Mobile . . . .
. . . . Email . . . .
. . . . Pager . . . .
. . . . Fax . . . .

Name . . . . Telephone . . . .
Address. . . . . Mobile . . . .
. . . . Email . . . .
. . . . Pager . . . .
. . . . Fax . . . .

Name . . . . Telephone . . . .
Address. . . . . Mobile . . . .
. . . . Email . . . .
. . . . Pager . . . .
. . . . Fax . . . .

Addresses

Name . . . .   Telephone . . . .
Address. . . . .   Mobile . . . .
. . . .   Email . . . .
. . . .   Pager . . . .
. . . .   Fax . . . .

Name . . . .   Telephone . . . .
Address. . . . .   Mobile . . . .
. . . .   Email . . . .
. . . .   Pager . . . .
. . . .   Fax . . . .

Name . . . .   Telephone . . . .
Address. . . . .   Mobile . . . .
. . . .   Email . . . .
. . . .   Pager . . . .
. . . .   Fax . . . .

Name . . . .   Telephone . . . .
Address. . . . .   Mobile . . . .
. . . .   Email . . . .
. . . .   Pager . . . .
. . . .   Fax . . . .

Name . . . .   Telephone . . . .
Address. . . . .   Mobile . . . .
. . . .   Email . . . .
. . . .   Pager . . . .
. . . .   Fax . . . .

Name . . . .   Telephone . . . .
Address. . . . .   Mobile . . . .
. . . .   Email . . . .
. . . .   Pager . . . .
. . . .   Fax . . . .

Addresses

Name . . . .   Telephone . . . .
Address . . . .   Mobile . . . .
. . . .   Email . . . .
. . . .   Pager . . . .
. . . .   Fax . . . .

Name . . . .   Telephone . . . .
Address . . . .   Mobile . . . .
. . . .   Email . . . .
. . . .   Pager . . . .
. . . .   Fax . . . .

Name . . . .   Telephone . . . .
Address . . . .   Mobile . . . .
. . . .   Email . . . .
. . . .   Pager . . . .
. . . .   Fax . . . .

Name . . . .   Telephone . . . .
Address . . . .   Mobile . . . .
. . . .   Email . . . .
. . . .   Pager . . . .
. . . .   Fax . . . .

Name . . . .   Telephone . . . .
Address . . . .   Mobile . . . .
. . . .   Email . . . .
. . . .   Pager . . . .
. . . .   Fax . . . .

Name . . . .   Telephone . . . .
Address . . . .   Mobile . . . .
. . . .   Email . . . .
. . . .   Pager . . . .
. . . .   Fax . . . .

Addresses

Name. . . . .
Telephone . . . .
Address. . . . .
Mobile . . . .
. . . .
Email . . . .
. . . .
Pager . . . .
. . . .
Fax . . . .

Name. . . . .
Telephone . . . .
Address. . . . .
Mobile . . . .
. . . .
Email . . . .
. . . .
Pager . . . .
. . . .
Fax . . . .

Name. . . . .
Telephone . . . .
Address. . . . .
Mobile . . . .
. . . .
Email . . . .
. . . .
Pager . . . .
. . . .
Fax . . . .

Name. . . . .
Telephone . . . .
Address. . . . .
Mobile . . . .
. . . .
Email . . . .
. . . .
Pager . . . .
. . . .
Fax . . . .

Name. . . . .
Telephone . . . .
Address. . . . .
Mobile . . . .
. . . .
Email . . . .
. . . .
Pager . . . .
. . . .
Fax . . . .

Name. . . . .
Telephone . . . .
Address. . . . .
Mobile . . . .
. . . .
Email . . . .
. . . .
Pager . . . .
. . . .
Fax . . . .

Printed by Firefly Books Ltd.
3680 Victoria Park Avenue, Toronto, Ontario M2H 3K1

Produced by Global Book Publishing Pty Ltd
1/181 High Street, Willoughby, NSW 2068, Australia
Ph +61 2 9967 3100 Fax +61 2 9967 5891
Email: rightsmanager@globalpub.com.au

First published in 2003

ISBN 1 55297 841 9

Printed in Hong Kong by Sing Cheong Printing Co. Ltd
Film separation by Pica Digital Pte Ltd, Singapore